CW00346922

Orphans, Widows, the Poor and Oppressed

Discover God's Heart for the Needy

Derek Prince

Orphans, Widows, the Poor and Oppressed

Copyright © 2006 by Derek Prince Ministries–International

This edition published by Derek Prince Ministries–UK 2006
This is edited from a transcript of a message given by Derek
Prince at Kensington Temple, London, in November 1999.
First published in 2000 Derek Prince Ministries–International

All rights reserved.

No part of this publication may be reproduced, stored in a
retrieval system, or transmitted, in any form or by any means,
electronic, mechanical, photocopying, recording or otherwise,
without the prior permission of the publisher.

ISBN: 1-901144-30-5
Product code: B46

All Scriptures are taken from The New King James Version
(NKJV). Copyright © 1979, 1980 1982 Thomas Nelson, Inc.,
Publishers.

Editorial, design and production services by Summit
Publishing Ltd.
Printed in the United Kingdom by Creative Print and Design
(Wales), Ebbw Vale.

1 2 3 4 5 6 7 8 9 10 / 09 08 07 06

Derek Prince Ministries—UK
Kingsfield, Hadrian Way, Baldock, SG7 6AN
www.dpmuk.org

Contents

Derek Prince   4

Introduction   5

The Nature of God   7

Requirements for Righteousness   9

The Sins of Sodom   19

In the New Testament   21

General Promises and Warnings   27

Personal Glimpses   31

Your Response   34

Committing Yourself to Caring   37

Derek Prince (1915-2003) was born in Bangalore, India, into a British military family. He was educated as a scholar of classical languages at Eton College and Cambridge University in England and later at Hebrew University, Israel. As a student, he was a philosopher and self-proclaimed atheist.

While in the British Medical Corps during World War II, Prince began to study the Bible as a philosophical work. Converted through a powerful encounter with Jesus Christ, he was baptized in the Holy Spirit a few days later. This life-changing experience altered the whole course of his life, which he thereafter devoted to studying and teaching the Bible as the Word of God.

Discharged from the army in Jerusalem in 1945, he married Lydia Christensen, founder of a children's home there. Upon their marriage, he immediately became father to Lydia's eight adopted daughters—six Jewish, one Palestinian Arab, one English. Together the family saw the rebirth of the state of Israel in 1948.

Lydia Prince died in 1975, and Derek married Ruth Baker, (a single mother to three adopted children) in 1978. He met his second wife, like his first, while he was serving the Lord in Jerusalem. Ruth died in December 1998 in Jerusalem where they had lived since 1981.

Derek Prince taught and ministered on six continents for over seven decades. In 2002 he said, "It is my desire—and I believe the Lord's desire—that this ministry continue the work, which God began through me over sixty years ago, until Jesus returns."

Derek Prince Ministries is now an international organisation which continues to impact lives by providing important Bible teaching to equip the worldwide church. His teaching has been translated into more than 60 languages and is equally relevant and helpful to people from all racial and religious backgrounds.

Introduction

I believe God has put on my heart something that can be a key to release the people of God into a much fuller outreach than many of them are in at this time. The subject is our responsibility as Christians for orphans, widows, the poor and the oppressed.

Many people speak about widows and orphans, but the Bible always puts it the other way around—orphans and widows—because orphans are totally helpless; widows are only partially helpless. And the Bible has much more to say about this than most of us have been aware. I have been preaching for over fifty years and I really have never seen this theme as I've been seeing it in the last few weeks and months.

In 1928 my first wife, Lydia, a Dane, began a small children's home in Jerusalem. She took in a little, dying Jewish baby. Having nothing to put her in, Lydia emptied her suitcase, wrapped the baby in her underwear, and began to care for her. This story is told in her book, *Appointment in Jerusalem*. It is a very dramatic, true story of how that happened. I'm proud that she was my wife.

I want to look at our responsibility for orphans, widows, the poor and oppressed in a systematic way. To begin with I want to study, first of all, the nature of God Himself. And then the requirements for righteousness in every successive stage of God's dealings, from the flood of Noah onwards—under the patriarchs, under the Law of Moses, under the prophets, in the New Testament, and then some general promises and warnings at the end.

The Nature of God

First of all, let's look at the nature of God Himself. In Psalm 68:5 it says of God:

> *A father of the fatherless, a defender of widows,*
> *Is God in His holy habitation?*

That is the character of God. He is a father to the fatherless and a defender to the widows.

Then in Psalm 103:6 it says:

> *The LORD executes righteousness*
> *And justice for all who are oppressed.*

I don't think most of us realize how passionately God cares for those who are oppressed. Most of the human race at this particular time is oppressed. The number of people who get a fair deal and are treated honourably is a small proportion of the human race. Most of the human race today is unjustly and unfairly treated. God cares about them. He loves them. He wants to help them, and He's also very, very angry with those who oppress them.

And then in Psalm 140:12:

> *I know that the LORD will maintain*
> *The cause of the afflicted,*
> *And justice for the poor.*

It is God's nature to care for the afflicted and to desire justice for the poor. And let's face it: frankly, there are not many places where the poor really get justice—certainly not in Britain or America.

Requirements for Righteousness

Now we will look at a picture of God's standard of righteousness in all the main ages that the Bible deals with, beginning with the age of the patriarchs (that is, the time before the Law of Moses). The time of Abraham, Isaac and Jacob and the time even earlier than that.

The Patriarchs

The main book that unfolds God's standard of righteousness is the book of Job, which is a very fascinating, stimulating and challenging book. In Job 29, Job himself gives us a picture of his righteousness. I found it extremely challenging to consider the way Job treated people. Job 29:11–13 says:

> *When the ear heard, then it blessed me,*
> *And when the eye saw, then it approved me; [in*
> *   other words I had favour with people. Why?]*
> *Because I delivered the poor who cried out,*
> *The fatherless and him who had no helper.*
> *The blessing of a perishing man came upon me,*
> *And I caused the widow's heart to sing for joy.*

Whom is he speaking about? The fatherless, the widows, the poor and the oppressed. Then he makes this remarkable statement, for those who are interested in doctrine:

> *I put on righteousness, and it clothed me;*
> *My justice was like a robe and a [diadem or] turban.*
> Job 29:14

None of us has righteousness of our own. All the way back to the time of Job he says, "I put on righteousness, and it clothed me." Every one of us who is counted righteous before God in any age is clothed with the righteousness which is not ours. We have no righteousness of our own. Back in the patriarchal time Job says, "I put on righteousness [not my own], and it clothed me." This is how his righteousness was expressed:

> I was eyes to the blind,
> And I was feet to the lame.
> I was a father to the poor,
> And I searched out the case that I did not know.
> I broke the fangs of the wicked,
> And plucked the victim from his teeth.
>   Job 29:15–17

Look at the outline of Job's righteousness. He says, "I delivered the poor, the fatherless, and the one who had no helper. The blessing of a perishing man came upon me. I caused the widow's heart to sing for joy." I wonder if you could ever say that. Have you ever done anything for a widow that would cause her heart to sing for joy? Widows are not far away. We'll look at that a little later.

Then, in Job 31, Job is asserting his righteousness before God. In doing so, he disclaims being guilty of various sins and he lists a number of sins that he did not commit. What impresses me is some of the things that he considered sinful. I want to take you to just one passage in Job 31. You must remember that these things are things that Job said he did not do because they were sinful. If he had been doing these things, he would not have expected any mercy from God.

"If I have kept the poor from their desire,
Or caused the eyes of the widow to fail,
Or eaten my morsel by myself,
So that the fatherless could not eat of it . . ."
                    Job 31:16–17

All those things Job considered sinful: to cause the eyes of the widow to fail, to eat your food by yourself when there were hungry people around. Job said he had never been guilty of that. Could you say that?

Then he goes on:

"(But from my youth I reared him [the fatherless] as
*   a father,*
And from my mother's womb I guided the widow);
If I have seen anyone perish for lack of clothing,
Or any poor man without covering . . . "
                    Job 31:18–19

"If I've seen anybody in need of clothing and did nothing about it," he says, *"that was sinful."*

Then he says:

"If his heart has not blessed me,
And if he was not warmed with the fleece of my sheep . . ."
                    Job 31:20

When Job saw a man who needed clothing, he took his own sheep, sheared them, and gave him the wool. Bear in mind, if Job had not done these things he would have considered himself a sinner.

He goes on:

"If I have raised my hand against the fatherless,
When I saw I had help in the gate [in the court];
Then let my arm fall from my shoulder,
Let my arm be torn from the socket."
                    Job 31:21–22

This is a tremendous statement! Do you understand what he is saying? He is saying, *"If I haven't used this arm of mine to bless the needy, to help the widows, to feed the hungry then it has no right to be on my body. It shouldn't be here."* Could you talk like that? Or does Job have a standard of righteousness which is different from most of ours today? And who is right—Job or us?

I get so challenged by these words. I have read them again and again and I've said to myself, this man Job had a standard of righteousness which we don't even think of today. And yet, he was affirming his righteousness before God.

The Law of Moses
Let's go on and look at the law of Moses. Leviticus 19:9–10 talks about how to handle your agriculture:

> *"'When you reap the harvest of your land, you shall not wholly reap the corners of your field, nor shall you gather the gleanings of your harvest.*
> *And you shall not glean your vineyard, nor shall you gather every grape of your vineyard . . .'"*

In other words you are to leave a certain amount of your harvest, whether it is corn or grapes, unreaped. Why?

> *"'you shall leave them for the poor and the stranger: I am the LORD your God.'"*

That was built into the law of Moses. Every Jew

that followed that law had to have concern for the poor and the stranger. It was part of his agricultural proceeding and they were agricultural people.

The Lord concludes there by saying, "I am the LORD your God." I interpret that this way: "This is the kind of God I am and this is how I want you to represent Me—with a concern for the poor and the stranger that's built into your whole life system and is part of it."

In Deuteronomy 14:28–29, it tells about a celebration that took place every third year. Speaking to all the people of Israel:

> "At the end of every third year you shall bring out the tithe of your produce of that year and store it up within your gates.
>
> And the Levite, because he has no portion nor inheritance with you . . ."

The Levite was the only one serving God and he did not have any inheritance because inheritance was the offering of God's people. So it would correspond to the missionary or the evangelist in our society today.

> "And the Levite, because he has no portion nor inheritance with you, and the stranger and the fatherless and the widow who are within your gates, may come and eat and be satisfied . . ."

You can see whom God cares for: the stranger, the fatherless and the widows. He has built it into the law. An Israelite could not follow the Law of Moses without being concerned for the stranger, the fatherless, and the widows.

And then God says that He is "the LORD your God." In other words, "That's the way I think; that's the way I am; that's how I want you to represent Me."

The Prophets

We come now to the prophets, and I will take just a few passages out of many. As I have studied the prophets over the years, I have come to certain conclusions. I will just share them with you and you can ask yourself if you agree.

I find, if you read the prophets from Isaiah onwards, basically there were three sins that provoked God's anger. The first was idolatry, the second was adultery and the third was indifference to the poor. In dealing with people over the years in deliverance, I have observed that if people get into idolatry it will often be followed by adultery. In other words, spiritual adultery leads to physical adultery. I have seen that time and time again.

We are all supposed to be shocked by idolatry and adultery. But what about the third thing that God puts on the same level? Indifference to the poor. This is what He says:

> *"Wash yourselves, make yourselves clean;*
> *Put away the evil of your doings from before My*
>   *eyes.*
> *Cease to do evil,*
> *Learn to do good;*
> *Seek justice,*
> *Rebuke the oppressor;*
> *Defend the fatherless,*
> *Plead for the widow."*
>   Isaiah 1:16

Who is at the top of God's list? The fatherless and the widow. God puts the failure to do that in the same category with idolatry and adultery. A little further on, speaking about the leaders of the people at that time, God says to Israel:

> *"Your princes are rebellious,*
> *And companions of thieves;*

Everyone loves bribes,
And follows after rewards.
They do not defend the fatherless.
Nor does the cause of the widow come before them."
Isaiah 1:23

Failure to defend the fatherless is in the same category as idolatry and adultery. Each of us has our own little list of sins, but they are very incomplete lists. I have been Pentecostal for many years and I've heard many wonderful sermons. But I never heard a sermon that clearly defines our responsibility to care for the orphans and the widows—never once in fifty-eight years.

When this really struck me, I said to myself, "How is it that I've been a preacher all these years and I've never seen this?" I'll tell you about my own personal experience a little later.

Going on, in Isaiah chapter 11 there is a prophecy of Jesus as the Messiah.

There shall come forth a Rod from the stem of Jesse,
And a Branch shall grow out of his roots.
The Spirit of the LORD *shall rest upon Him,*
The Spirit of wisdom and understanding,
The Spirit of counsel and might,
The Spirit of knowledge and of the fear of the LORD.
His delight is in the fear of the LORD,
And He shall not judge by the sight of His eyes,
Nor decide by the hearing of His ears;
But with righteousness He shall judge the poor,
And decide with equity for the meek of the earth . . .
Isaiah 11:1–4a

Whom is Jesus concerned about? The poor, the meek, the

oppressed, the people that don't get a fair deal.

Personally, I come from a privileged level of society in Britain. I'm not speaking about what I didn't get because I got a lot more than I should have gotten. But I have come to realize that most of the people in this country are not really getting what they should. That may shock you, but I find it is true. The basic reason for this is human selfishness. Everybody cares for himself. Do you know you can be Pentecostal and very selfish? You can speak in tongues and be very self-centred, very concerned about yourself. I believe in speaking in tongues; I speak in tongues every day. But that's not a substitute for my character.

Isaiah 58 is a passage that David Wilkerson calls "the key to continuing revival." The record of his ministry probably justifies his claim. Isaiah 58:6:

> *"Is this not the fast that I have chosen:*
> *To loose the bonds of wickedness . . ."*

I believe in fasting. Basically, I fast every week. So I am not suggesting that fasting is unimportant, but God says there's a lot more to fasting than just abstaining from food.

> *"To loose the bonds of wickedness,*
> *To undo the heavy burdens,*
> *To let the oppressed go free,*
> *And that you break every yoke?*
> *Is it not to share your bread with the hungry,*
> *And that you bring to your house the poor who are cast*
>   *out;*
> *When you see the naked, that you cover him,*
> *And not hide yourself from your own flesh?"*
>   Isaiah 58:6–7

Are we guilty of not seeing the people who need us? Do

you know where they are? It is really a refusal to identify yourself with your people. In the major cities in the USA, the poor have moved into central areas creating ghettos. Meanwhile, the wealthy have moved out to the suburbs. What is that? It is hiding yourself from your own people. It is refusing to confront the need of your people.

Then comes this wonderful promise:

> *"When you see the naked, that you cover him,*
> *And not hide yourself from your own flesh?*
> *Then your light shall break forth like the morning,*
> *Your healing shall spring forth speedily,*
> *And your righteousness shall go before you;*
> *The glory of the* LORD *shall be your rear guard.*
> *Then you shall call, and the* LORD *will answer;*
> *You shall cry, and He will say, 'Here I am.' "*
> Isaiah 58:7b–9

Here is a guarantee of answered prayer. But it is on the condition that you care for the people who are in need — *"that you do not hide yourself from your own flesh."*

I was educated at Eton and then at Cambridge and I was put in a segment of society that just did not recognize there were people that needed help. It wasn't exactly that we were against them; we were just indifferent. Then I was called up into the British Army in 1940 and I was suddenly pitched forth into a lot of people I had never known existed. Especially the Geordies, whom I love. They are warm-hearted people. But when I went into the British Army, I couldn't understand them and they couldn't understand me. Literally, we did not have a language in which to communicate. And I began to discover there are different people in Britain that I had never known. I never knew anything about them. I was confronted with a lot of areas in my own character that needed dealing with. I'd been *hiding myself from my own flesh.* I could have had an easy way through life probably the rest of my life. I'll tell you how it changed a little later.

The Sins of Sodom

Now I want to talk about Sodom for a moment. A lot of people think they know what the real sin of Sodom was. It was homosexuality, wasn't it? But that's not what God charges it with. This amazed me when I discovered it. Ezekiel 16 is addressed to the city of Jerusalem, but it compares Jerusalem with Sodom. And this is what the Lord says about Sodom:

"Look, this was the iniquity of your sister Sodom: She and her daughter [that's her fellow cities] had pride, fullness of food, and abundance of idleness; neither did she strengthen the hand of the poor and needy."
Ezekiel 16:49

There is no mention of homosexuality. I don't mean that God is indifferent toward homosexuality, far from it. But the basic sins of Sodom were selfishness, carnality, self-indulgence, looking after "Number One." And do you know what I believe? This is just my opinion, but I believe that kind of culture will always produce homosexuality. That is why we have so many homosexuals in the world today, because the sins of our day are just like the sins of Sodom. Let's read them again:

"Look, this was the iniquity of your sister Sodom: She and her daughter had pride, fullness of food, and abundance of idleness; neither did she strengthen the hand of the poor and needy."

How well does that describe our contemporary culture? Now, there are wonderful exceptions to this, but they are exceptions. We can lament the upsurge of homosexuality, but I believe that kind of culture will always produce homosexuality. Homosexuality is not the root. The root is selfishness, self-indulgence, indifference to others.

In the New Testament

Let's turn to the New Testament, to Luke's gospel. Again, this is something that so impacted me I really had to decide what I was going to do about it. And I haven't decided yet. This is part of the ministry of John the Baptist who, as you know, was sent to be the forerunner to prepare the way for Jesus. His theme was summed up in one word—repentance. In Luke 3 John says this:

> *"And even now the axe is laid to the root of the trees. Therefore every tree which does not bear good fruit is cut down and thrown into the fire."*
> Luke 3:9

Notice, God requires good fruit. It is not enough to say that you don't bear bad fruit or that you're not doing anything wrong. But, are you bearing good fruit? Because if you're not, it'll be cut down and thrown into the fire. Notice this is not addressed to the prostitutes or the tax collectors, but to everybody. They heard his message.

> *So the people asked him, saying, "What shall we do then?" [What have we got to do? His answer was so simple.] He answered and said to them, "He who has two tunics, let him give to him who has none; and he who has food, let him do likewise."*
> Luke 3:10–11

Not complicated, not theology—just be concerned about the people who need you. When I read that, I got a mental picture of all the suits and the jackets I have hanging in various wardrobes in various places. And I thought to myself, *I don't need all those.* It's not that I am greedy and I don't amass clothing. It just somehow grows. I live in three different countries at different times of the year and it gets complicated. But I thought to myself, *I have never acted on that word ever in my life.*

If you have two jackets and somebody else none, what do you do? You give it to him. If you have food and somebody else has none, what do you do? You give it to him. So we're clear what that means.

Then in Luke 14 Jesus gives instructions. He had been invited to the house of a Pharisee for a meal. At the end of the meal He gives this advice to the Pharisee.

> *Then He also said to him who invited Him, "When you give a dinner or a supper, do not ask your friends, your brothers, your relatives, nor rich neighbours, lest they also invite you back, and you be repaid.*
> *"But when you give a feast, invite the poor, the maimed, the lame, the blind.*
> *"And you will be blessed, because they cannot repay you; for you shall be repaid at the resurrection of the just."*
> Luke 14:12–14

That is a general statement to Christians. When you have a party, whom are you going to invite? Your friends, your relatives, or the people who really need the invitation who can't invite you back? I want you to see this as consistent all through the Bible. It is not something that just comes up in one place. I am amazed that I have studied the Bible so long and never saw it so clearly as I have seen it in the last few weeks.

In 1957 when I was living at number 77 Westbourne Grove, at about two o'clock in the morning the Lord woke me up and He spoke to me audibly. I could take you to the place where I was, the place where the Lord was standing, although

I didn't see Him. This is what He said: "There shall be a great revival in the United States and Great Britain." And I noticed how polite the Lord was. He calls everybody the right title. The United States and Great Britain. Not just "Britain," but "Great Britain." I believe it is very near. It is coming very soon, not because we have earned it, but because God decided to send it. Then He said this to me (and I very rarely say this, but I feel God wants me to): "Thou shalt be His instrument in Britain, but the condition is obedience in small things and in great things. For the small things are as great as the great things."

I really believe this message is the key to releasing revival in Britain. You've got thousands of wonderful Christians who just sit in church chairs and sing hymns. What about the people who really need you? You don't even have contact with them, some of you. If you were told today to invite the poor, the maimed, the lame and the blind, you wouldn't know who to invite. You are so far removed from them, you're just not in contact. But they are the people who need you.

In Matthew 25 we find the prophetic parable of the sheep and the goat nations. We can't go into this in detail but it is a picture of the end of the age. When the Lord establishes His kingdom, He's going to judge the nations and there will be two categories—the sheep and the goats. The sheep He'll set on His right hand; the goats on His left. The sheep He will invite into His kingdom; the goats He will reject totally. To the goat nations He pronounces some of the most terrible words that ever came from His lips.

> "Then He will also say to those on the left hand [the goats], 'Depart from Me, you cursed, into the everlasting fire prepared for the devil and his angels . . .' "
> Matthew 25:41

What terrible words to hear proceeding from the mouth of the Lord!

The everlasting fire was never prepared for human beings, but the devil has no option. It is where he is going to end. We don't have to end there; we have a choice. Then Jesus tells them why:

> "'... for I was hungry and you gave Me no food; I was thirsty and you gave Me no drink;
> 'I was a stranger and you did not take Me in, naked and you did not clothe Me, sick and in prison and you did not visit Me.'
> "Then they also will answer Him, saying, 'Lord, when did we see You hungry or thirsty or a stranger or naked or sick or in prison, and did not minister to You?'
>
> "Then He will answer them, saying, 'Assuredly, I say to you, inasmuch as you did not do it to one of the least of these, you did not do it to Me.'"
> Matthew 25:42–45

Bear in mind that we can go to an everlasting condemnation for the things we *have not* done. Not for the things we have done. He didn't condemn them for what they had done. He condemned them for what they had not done. It is a very solemn thought.

My personal view of contemporary Western (Christianized) culture, is that we will be judged not for what we have done, but for what we *have not* done. There are no exceptions. We are going to be judged not so much for the sins we have committed, although that will be part of it, but for the good things we didn't do. I have not read anywhere in the Bible more terrible words than these: "Inasmuch as you did not do it . . . Depart from Me, you cursed, into the everlasting fire prepared for the devil and his angels."

This is all summed up in a couple of verses in the epistle

of James and it summarizes the teaching of the New Testament. It says:

Pure and undefiled religion before God and the Father is this: to visit [care for] orphans and widows in their trouble, and to keep oneself unspotted from the world.
James 1:27

Being an old-time Pentecostal, I have heard many, many sermons about not being like the world. Sermons were preached against worldliness and all sorts of things that were classified as worldliness. But I never heard a sermon on our responsibility for orphans and widows. Never. I've heard some very fine preaching in my days. But James says that this is pure and undefiled religion before God and the Father.

There is a negative side to this: *keep oneself unspotted from the world*. But the positive takes precedence: *to care for the orphans and widows*. Are you practising that kind of religion? If not, who exempted you? Who decided that you were not included in this? I'll tell you one thing: it applies to me.

———⚙※———

General Promises and Warnings

Now let's look at a few general statements, mainly from the book of Proverbs.

> *He who has pity on the poor lends to the LORD,*
> *And He will pay back what he has given.*
> Proverbs 19:17

So when you give to the poor you're lending to the Lord. I'll tell you one thing, the Lord always pays back. He never remains indebted. How much have you given? Stop and ask yourself. You pay your tithe. That's wonderful, but that's only the beginning. It is a very important beginning but it's not all.

I am really happy to think about what I have given to the poor. I am not claiming to be a great giver, but I'm glad to know that the Lord is going to pay me back. I trust Him. I have lent to people who did not pay me back. If you've had the same experience, the one person who will pay you back is the Lord. Here's a word of advice: never lend to members of your family, just give it.

Proverbs 31 describes the excellent wife, the model mother.

> *She extends her hand to the poor,*
> *Yes, she reaches out her hands to the needy.*
> Proverbs 31:20

Dear married lady, is that true of you? Why not? Does it apply? You have to answer, I don't.

Then there are two warnings.

Whoever shuts his ears to the cry of the poor
Will also cry himself and not be heard.
Proverbs 21:13

Is that the reason why some of our prayers are not answered, because we haven't heard the cry of the poor? If we don't hear the cry of the poor, God will not hear our cry.

He who gives to the poor will not lack,
But he who hides his eyes will have many curses.
Proverbs 28:27

For those of you who are familiar with the Middle East, that is certainly true. When a beggar stretches out his hand and you give him nothing he will follow you down the street with his curses. Those curses really have some power, they are not just words.

My first wife lived among the people of Jerusalem, speaking mainly Arabic. She went into a shop in the Old City and the man wanted to sell her something and she said it was too expensive. She wouldn't buy it. She said as she walked out down the street she stumbled and almost fell. She realized the shopkeeper had put a curse on her. Believe me, dear brothers and sisters, don't venture in the Middle East if you don't understand the power of blessings and curses, because they are very powerful.

One final picture of a good Charismatic meeting, described in Amos chapter 6. The main theme of the book of Amos is injustice and selfishness. And for those reasons, a whole nation was banished from the presence of God.

Woe to you who put far off the day of doom,
Who cause the seat of violence to come near;

Who lie on beds of ivory,
Stretch out on your couches,
Eat lambs from the flock
And calves from the midst of the stall;
Who sing idly to the sound of stringed instruments,
And invent for yourselves musical instruments
    like David;
Who drink wine from bowls [now most of you don't
    do that],
And anoint yourselves with the best ointments,
But are not grieved for the affliction of Joseph.
                Amos 6:3–6

Doesn't that sound like a Charismatic meeting? We have a good time. There is a lot of music, we eat, and we are really happy. But we will not be concerned about the people who don't have anything. That is not true of all, but it is true of many. I don't say that to condemn you, but if you really want the blessing of the Lord on yourself and on this nation, you are going to have to do something about it.

Personal Glimpses

You might say, "Brother Prince, you've preached a lot. What have you done?" So I'm going to tell you and I want to say I take no credit for this whatever. I didn't do it because I was good or righteous, but because the Lord showed me to do it.

I was born in India of a British family, an only child, educated at Eton and Cambridge. I was born, as they say, with a silver spoon in my mouth. And then I went into the British Army, reluctantly, and I ended up in the Middle East. There I met a Danish lady, Lydia, much older than I was, who had started a little children's home. I fell in love with her and I felt that God wanted me to marry her. God also told Lydia He wanted me to marry her. So when I married her, the same day I got a wife, I got eight daughters! Remember, I was an only child. I never had a sister and didn't know much about women. Six of the children were Jewish, one was Arab, and one was English.

I'll tell you a little about them, starting with the youngest. My youngest, who is English, married a Goan, if you know what a Goan is. A Goan is a man from Goa, an Indian territory. She has two children—a son and a daughter. So that gives me two grandchildren.

Then there is my Arab daughter, married to an Englishman. She has three children and one grandchild. So that gives me three grandchildren and one great-grandchild.

But now wait for the punch line! One of my Jewish daughters, Magdal, married a widower, who is a minister of the gospel. He already had six children by his first wife who passed away, and she had five more. So that gives me eleven grandchildren. Magdal has twenty-eight grandchildren. So I have twenty-eight great-grand children. And that's not the end by any means! We can go two generations further. So I am not without experience.

You might say, "Well, what did you do?" I really can't take the credit for it but, first of all, I fell in love, and then I fell in love with the family. Out of that family, which started with one little desperately sick Jewish baby in 1928, there is a family that now has more than one hundred and fifty members. We are distributed around the world from Israel to Britain to Canada to the United States to Australia. But, marvel of all marvels, we really are one family. Every one of us would agree. We have never been divided. We have never split up. That is the grace of God. I take no credit for it, but I give God all the credit.

So I got eight children initially in my first marriage. Then Lydia and I went out to Africa, to Kenya, to do an educational work. For five years I was a principal of a college for training African teachers for African schools.

One day, about five o'clock in the evening, a rather strangely assorted group of people turned up—a white lady carrying a little black baby in nothing but a dirty towel and a black African couple. They said, "This little baby's mother died in giving birth. The infant was found on the floor of an African hut. Somebody picked her up and took her to the hospital, where she's been for six months. Now the hospital says they are not a children's home and can't keep babies. So we have been looking for three days in this whole area for any family—African, Asian or European—that will take this little baby. We went to the mission hospital and they said they couldn't take her but said 'the Princes take children.' " That was why they came to us.

"Well," we said, "that was long ago. We don't do that now. And we have our own work that keeps us busy from morning till night."

"We're so tired," they said. "Would you let us sit down?" So we offered them seats and gave them a glass of water to drink. After about fifteen or twenty minutes, they got up to go.

As the white lady walked past me she paused just for a moment, not for any special reason. And this little black baby put out her left hand like that towards me as if to say, "What are you going to do about me?" And I looked at my wife who was right on the other side of the room. Normally, we would pray about something like that before we would make a decision. And bless her, Lydia said, "Give me a week to get a crib and some baby clothes and you can bring her back." So that's how we got our ninth child.

Then when I married Ruth I got three more Jewish children, adopted by her and her first husband. So I have twelve children—eleven girls and one boy.

I used to say to Ruth, "One thing you cannot complain about is our life being dull." And it never has been dull. Since I came to know the Lord I have never had a dull life. I have faced challenges and opportunities and needs I didn't even know existed.

Your Response

Now the question is, if you believe what I've said is right, what are you going to do about it? Are you going to do anything? Let me tell you one thing that most of us could do. I have in my heart a real burden for single mothers. When I married Ruth she was a single mother with three children. Her husband had deserted her. And I want to tell you that most single mothers have a very difficult time. Some of you know that from personal experience.

I believe the Church has an obligation. I said this to a brother once and he said, "Well, it's their sin that got them into that trouble." That is not really the truth. It is a fact that some of them were unwed mothers, but not most of them. But even if they were, where in the gospel does Jesus forbid us to show mercy to sinners? After all, they need mercy. But most of them are left struggling with a situation that they're not really guilty for. I believe the Church can do something for single mothers.

Let me say this to you: the key to happiness is not being loved, it is having someone to love. That's what makes life exciting. And there are people not very far from you who need your love. They may not be very lovable people. In fact, they may be a little bit bitter, a little bit angry, a little bit against God, saying, "He hasn't treated me right. Why am I in this situation?" But I want to tell you, if you really want to be happy, find somebody to love. It will make all the difference in your life. It is wonderful to be loved. I am loved by many people though I don't deserve it. But I tell you what really brings joy to my heart is to love somebody who is not loved, and to see the smile on their face when they say, "At last, I've got a friend."

You see, selfishness is a key to misery. You can be very spiritual, very committed, and still be pretty miserable. So I want to suggest that we need to think of what we are going to do about single mothers. To most of you who have homes and families, here is a challenge. Not very far from you somewhere, there is a single mother who would benefit from your help. One thing that is difficult for women is taking care of a car. It is difficult for me, too. There are all sorts of things that I don't understand about cars. I have been privileged to have sons-in-law who understand cars, so I don't have to worry. But for a woman on her own, it is a struggle to be responsible for a car. Yet her job and her life may depend on having a car. If you could help her, you would have a friend. Don't be religious or start to tell her you want to win her to the Lord. Just say, "I've seen you're having a difficult time. Maybe I can help you." And after a little while, something will change in her heart and in her children.

I just finished writing a book called *Husbands and Fathers*. My diagnosis of the problem of the Western world is renegade fathers—fathers who have reneged on their primary responsibilities as husbands and fathers. The result is chaos in society. You can have all sorts of social programmes but there is no substitute for God's way. And God's way is a family. Nobody has ever invented anything that will take the place of a family. It is a privilege to be part of a family. I thank God every day for my family. I pray for them and they pray for me. I am embarrassed to think how many people pray for me.

I had a physical problem diagnosed as cancer a little while ago. And I got letters from many different countries saying people were praying for me or their church was praying for me. I thought to myself, that's unreasonable. But I don't turn it down.

I am suggesting that some of you need to break loose from your little religious mould and do something daring. After all, I did it. How many people would marry a woman and get eight daughters at the same time? And I tell you it was the making of me. It got me out of the religious rut. It got me involved with real people and real problems.

I would like to give you an opportunity to make some kind of commitment. So I am going to ask you if you, having read this book, might want to pray this prayer:

"Lord, I'm not really fulfilled. I could do a lot more than I'm doing. In many ways I'm pretty self-centred, to tell the truth. But I would like to make myself available to You to love somebody else who isn't loved. To care for somebody who's not cared for."

Then give yourself to the Lord for whatever purpose He has in your life, to become a servant to others.

If having prayed this prayer you now feel challenged to actually **do** something, but do not know where to begin, read on—we have gleaned some useful information to assist you. This is not an exhaustive list but should help to get you started. The information contains both Christian and non-Christian organisations for we are told to be light in a dark world and simple acts of kindness say volumes about our faith in God.

Committing Yourself to Caring

Caring for Orphans and Other Needy Children
I was hungry and you gave Me food

Child sponsorship and overseas childcare programmes
There are a number of agencies helping children in desperate and needy situations. Statistics show that today 1.3 billion people live in extreme poverty. Tonight 800 million people will go to bed hungry. This year 12 million children will die before their fifth birthday. In the developing world, one child dies every 3 seconds because of the basic lack of safe water, healthcare, shelter or food—the things we often take for granted.

Ways that can assist aid agencies include: sending a gift to a needy child, speaking to church groups or running articles in church magazines. You could also encourage awareness by mobilising others to respond to the needs of needy children.

> *Christian Aid*, 35 Lower Marsh, Waterloo, London, SE1 7RL
> Phone: 0207 6204444 Email: info@christian-aid.org
> www.christian-aid.org.uk

> *Compassion UK*, 43 High Street, Weybridge, Surrey, KT13 8BB
> Phone: 01932 832253 Email: info@compassionuk.org
> www.compassionuk.org

> *Tearfund*, 100 Church Road, Teddington, TW11 8QE
> Phone: 0845 3558355 Email: enquiry@tearfund.org
> www.tearfund.org

> *World Vision UK*, Opal Drive, Fox Milne, Milton Keynes, MK15 0ZR
> Phone: 01908 841010 Email: info@worldvision.org.uk
> www.worldvision.org.uk

Give a gift of love
Another idea is to give a gift to the needy. Rather than receiving more unwanted birthday gifts, there are agencies who will arrange for a suitable gift to be given to someone in real need.

Living Generously, PO Box 112, Bristol, BS48 2XZ
Phone: 0870 9913635
www.livinggenerously.com

Listening and caring

Perhaps you could donate a few hours a week to a child who otherwise would not be getting much-needed educational and other support in the form of listening and talking? There are some after school groups attached to larger churches that provide this kind of help; could you offer your services? Maybe this is something your own church could start?

Organisations operating in this area often need help with holiday-time activities such as assisting in art, drama, sport, games and activity workshops. You could also get involved in cooking, minibus driving, computer supervision and socialising regularly with a member.

Other opportunities to help include: supporting fundraising, marketing, recruiting volunteers and administration work.

Chance UK (A London based mentoring organisation for children from 5—11 years old who are at risk of school or social exclusion)
Chance UK, Units S1-S2, 89-93 Fonthill Road, London, N4 3JH
Phone: 0207 2815858 Email: admin@chanceuk.comwww.chanceuk.com

Kith and Kids (A group who support children and adults with a range of disabilities)
Kith and Kids, The Irish Centre, Pretoria Road, London, N17 8DX
Phone: 0208 8017432 Email: projects@kithandkids.org.uk
www.kithandkids.org.uk

Helping families stay together

So many children are 'orphaned' by divorce. Have you a Marriage Help Programme in your church? Talk to your minister how you could get involved in starting one? Sometimes just listening can really save the day. If you find someone who is suffering in their marriage, try lending an ear. If you want to get more involved, you could try to help families stay together by training to be a counsellor.

Relate, Herbert Gray College, Little Church Street, Rugby, Warwickshire, CV21 3AP
Phone: 0845 4561310 or 01788 573241 Email: enquiries@relate.org.uk
www.relate.org.uk
For local details visit the website or your local telephone directory.

Pay for a deserving couple to take a break

Another idea is to sponsor a couple who you believe may need a little light relief in the form of a weekend away from their children.

Marriage Encounter, David and Liz Percival
11 Lamborne Close, Sandhurst, Berks, GU47 8JL
Phone: 01344 779658 Email: mail@marriageencounter.freeserve.co.uk
www.marriageencounter.freeserve.co.uk

Baptist Expression of Marriage Encounter
26 Bellingdon Road, Chesham, Bucks, HP5 2HA
Phone: 01494 782466 Email: billandben26@tiscali.co.uk
www.beofme.co.uk

Caring for Widows and Single Mothers
. . . to visit orphans and widows in their trouble

Helping a mum to cope

Seek out a single mother to help in your neighbourhood or church. Remember, single mothers are a type of widow and their children, a type of orphan. Offer to baby-sit so she can shop or get a short break from the pressures of being both a mother and a father. Invite her round for a meal with her children, be a friend by listening to her and trying to encourage her.

Home-Start UK, 2 Salisbury Road, Leicester, LE1 7QR
Phone: 0800 0686368 or 0116 2339955
Email: volunteering@home-start.org.uk www.home-start.org.uk

Helping a widow

The death of a partner is always a tragedy and even more so when it is a young person who is left on their own to cope with a family. Many men and women know at first hand the pain and devastation it causes when parents have to face helping their children through incredible grief while coping with their own distress. Many find it hard to go on.

Care for the Family, PO Box 488, Cardiff, CF15 7YY
Phone: 0292 0810800 Email: mail@cff.org.uk
www.careforthefamily.org.uk

Spending time with the elderly

Elderly people are often lonely and it is good to befriend an older person, especially when they have lost their partner. Could you offer this kind of friendship?

We spoke to someone who visits elderly people as a ministry and asked her for some pointers. She said, "The first time I visited an elderly person, I was nervous. I kept thinking, 'What if they are suspicious of my motives?' I spoke to the minister at my church who arranged for me to visit someone who had just been widowed. They knew I was coming as it had been arranged. When I knocked at the door, I simply said, 'I have come to visit you.' The recipient was very pleased and our friendship lasted for years."

Age Concern, Astral House, 1268 London Road,London, SW16 4ER
Phone: 0208 7657200 or 0800 009966 www.ageconcern.org.uk
For local details visit the website or your local telephone directory.

Sponsor an elderly person

Sponsor an elderly person. Many elderly women in the Third World have no means of support and die prematurely.

Help the Aged, 207-221 Pentonville Road, London, N1 9UZ
Phone: 0207 2781114 Email: info@helptheaged.org.uk
www.helptheaged.org.uk

Caring for the Poor
I was thirsty and you gave Me drink

Responding to disasters
Volunteer time or donate funds to national relief groups. As the number of natural disasters increase, these organisations are often the first to reach those who are without food or shelter.

VSO, Carlton House, 85 Upper Richmond Road, London, SW15 2BS
Phone: 0208 7807600 Email: infoservices@vso.org.uk www.vso.org.uk

Skillshare International, 126 New Walk, Leicester, LE1 7JA
Phone: 0116 2541862 Email: info@skillshare.org www.skillshare.org

RedR (Engineers for Disaster Relief maintains a register of professionals who can respond to short-term needs of relief agencies.)
RedR London, 1 Great George Street, London, SW1P 3AA
Phone: 0207 2333116 Email: info@redr.org www.redr.org/london

Youth With A Mission, Highfield Oval, Ambrose Lane, Harpenden, Herts, AL5 4BX
Phone: 01582 463300 Email: info@oval.com www.ywamharpenden.org

Operation Mobilisation, Global Challenge
The Quinta, Weston Rhyn, Oswestry, Shropshire, SY10 7LT
Phone: 01691 773388 Email: info@uk.om.org (General information)
Email: personnel@uk.om.org (Joining information) www.om.org

Mercy Ships UK, The Lighthouse, 12 Meadway Court,
Stevenage, Hertfordshire, SG1 2EF
Phone: 0870 8707447 Email: info@mercyships.org.uk
www.mercyships.org.uk

Inter-Cultural Youth Exchange, Latin America House,
Kingsgate Place, London, NW6 4TA
Phone: 0870 7743486 Email: manager@icye.org.uk www.icye.org.uk

International Voluntary Service (IVS), Old Hall, East Bergholt,
Colchester, CO7 6TQ
Phone: 01206 298215 Email: ivssouth@ivs-gb.org.uk www.ivs-gb.org.uk

Helping your neighbour

For families on the bread line, repairs to plumbing, heating or other home maintenance problems, are a huge headache. A great idea is to draw up a Church Helps list where the relevant skills can be held by the minister for such emergencies.

Reach out to a struggling family in your church or someone you know is having a hard time financially. Invite them to dinner or out to lunch. Help them with their needs at home or pay a bill for them. Encourage them in whatever way you can.

Offer to decorate a room for a family in need. The criteria for this is that you finish to the standard that you would have in your own home.

Another idea is to keep gift vouchers handy for clothes or food. Give them out as you come across people in need.

Give it away

Derek was challenged by Luke 3:10-11 where John the Baptist said the people should give their spare clothing to those in need. Likewise we can give our used clothing to a charity shop whose profits aid those in need. Go through your wardrobe and bag up those unnecessary items. Relief organisations such as Oxfam will be more than grateful for your efforts. Furniture and some white goods can be donated to Furniture Aid programmes. Look in your Yellow Pages or call your local council for information.

Oxfam Supporter Relations, Oxfam House, John Smith Drive, Cowley, Oxford, OX4 2JY
Phone: 0870 3332444 (General) Phone: 0845 3000311 (Shops)
www.oxfam.org.uk

Helping the homeless

Can you imagine how difficult life must be without a proper home? Perhaps you might consider helping an agency committed to this cause?

Shelter, 88 Old Street, London, EC1V 9HU
Phone: 0207 4906720 Email: training@shelter.org.uk
www.shelter.org.uk.

Caring for the Oppressed, the Afflicted, the Sick and Those Without Hope

I was sick and you visited Me
I was in prison and you came to Me

Invest in prison ministry.

The voluntary sector work is essential in supporting the prison system in offering support to families which is invaluable to the prisoners. It also helps the community as evidence has shown that prisoners who maintain strong family relationships are much less likely to offend.

Here are some of the areas that you could get involved in as part of a prison ministry:

Collecting toys and games for children's play areas; running safe play areas; running support groups for women; helping with administration; assisting with chaplaincy work; being an independent person involved in observing extended visits; serving refreshments; helping with father and child visits out; helping with Mother and Baby units; providing toiletries for new babies; providing listening ears and being on the Visitor's Centre Committee.

Derek Prince Ministries-UK offer free Bible teaching to prisoners as part of their Inside Outreach programme. The lives of more than 1,000 prisoners have been impacted through this programme over the last 10 years. If you would like to support this initiative then please contact the office or visit the website.

Mothers' Union, Mary Sumner House, 24 Tufton Street,
London, SW1P 3RB
Phone: 0207 2225533 Email: mu@themothersunion.org
www.themothersunion.org

Samaritans, The Upper Mill, Kingston Road, Ewell, Surrey, KT17 2AF
Phone: 0208 3948300 Email: admin@samaritans.org
www.samaritans.org

Another excellent source for help in coming alongside prisoners and their families, is to set up and run a course within a prison environment.

Alpha, Holy Trinity Brompton, Brompton Road, London, SW7 1JA
Phone: 0845 6447544 Email: info@alphacourse.org
www.uk.alphacourse.org/prisons

Helping those who are sick

Cancer is the UK's biggest killer. Every year it claims the lives of more than 150,000 people, with a further one million living with the disease at any one time. Help out by volunteering to assist with one of the many charities dedicated to this cause.

Marie Curie Cancer Care, 89 Albert Embankment, London, SE1 7TP
Phone: 0207 5997777 www.mariecurie.org.uk

If you want to volunteer your time to helping improve the lives of men, women and children challenged by HIV and AIDS there are agencies that would welcome you.

Mildmay Mission Hospital, Hackney Road, London, E2 7NA
Phone: 0207 6136300 Email: dave.windsor@mildmay.org
www.mildmay.org.uk

Coming alongside those suffering with depression and other problems

Depression is a common enough ailment, but often we feel so helpless to help someone who is feeling really low. Sometimes it's enough to simply come alongside someone suffering in this way. Listening is the key. If you believe this is an area that you could be useful in, why not invest in some training?

CWR, Waverley Abbey House, Waverley Lane, Farnham,
Surrey, GU9 8EP.
Phone: 01252 784700 Email: mail@cwr.org.uk www.cwr.org.uk

Association of Christian Counsellors, 29 Momus Boulevard,
Coventry, CV2 5NA,
Phone: 0845 1249569 Email: office@acc-uk.org www.acc-uk.org.

Another helpful agency with training is the *Samaritans*.
Contact: training@samaritans.org. (Full details on previous page.)

Offering encouragement

If you are not very mobile, being available on the end of a phone to lend a sympathetic ear to those in need is a very valuable source of help. Encouragement in the form of letter writing and sending cards is another great help. Contact your minister to let him or her know you are willing to help in this way.

Helping those with drug and addiction problems

There are many addiction and rehabilitation organisations which would welcome help, some in fund raising and others in raising awareness.

Teen Challenge London, Wilkerson House, Uphall Road, Ilford, Essex, IG1 2JJ
Phone: 0208 5533338 Email: info@teenchallenge.org.uk
www.teenchallenge.org.uk.

Hope UK (A Christian charity providing education and training for parents, churches and voluntary youth organisations.)
Hope UK, 25(F) Copperfield Street, London, SE1 0EN
Phone: 0207 9280848 Email: d.devine@hopeuk.org
www.hopeuk.org

Make this your proclamation:

I will seek justice and encourage the oppressed. I will defend the cause of the fatherless and plead the case of the widow.
(Personalised from Isaiah 1:17 NIV)

Although care has gone into the compilation of this information, DPM—UK would like to point out that we are not directly responsible for any external sites listed in this book.

Derek Prince Ministries

At Derek Prince Ministries, our primary mission and calling is to impact lives by providing Bible teaching to equip and build up the Church, all around the world. However, there are situations we occasionally come across, where we are faced with urgent practical needs, that are not already being addressed by relief organisations. DPM has been led on some of these occasions, to provide help for people's immediate physical needs, before then seeking to help with their spiritual needs.

In recent years this has involved:-

- Supporting 40 children in Ethiopia, orphaned because of HIV/Aids and assisting several widows who have no means of supporting themselves. We have provided food, clothes, shoes and made it possible for the children to receive a basic school education.

- Standing with persecuted believers in the Middle East, by helping to provide safe houses and food. Those that come to Christ, particularly from a Muslim background, often have to flee for their lives because of death threats from their own families.

- Providing practical assistance, in the aftermath of the Asian Tsunami in December 2004, through DPM contacts in the region. We helped rebuild houses, provide nets to fishermen, and sewing machines to widows, to give a means of ongoing self support.

- We have a mercy ministry in our Indian office, which is a practical demonstration of God's love to orphans in their area.

The coupon on the next page gives you the opportunity to join the DPM network, and get involved with the continuing work of Derek Prince Ministries.

Join the DPM Network and Receive a FREE
Derek Prince Ministries Audio Teaching

If you have enjoyed reading this book and are interested in going deeper into the Word of God, then join our informal network of individuals, pastors and lay leaders interested in learning how to grow in their faith and respond to challenges of daily life.

To join and receive the following teaching message FREE OF CHARGE, fill out this form and send in an envelope to our address below.

Mother in Israel by Lydia Prince

How would you respond if God called you to something radical? In this captivating message, Lydia Prince tells of how God took her from the classrooms of Denmark to a basement in Jerusalem. Her inspiring story will both amaze and challenge you.

Preferred format: ☐ CD ☐ Tape ☐ MP3* (Code: 8101)

* Please supply email address

Name _____

Address _____

_____Postcode _____

Tel _____

E-mail* _____

Role in the local church: ☐ Member ☐ Lay Leader ☐ Pastor ☐ None

Age: ☐ 18–25 ☐ 26–35 ☐ 36–45 ☐ 46–55 ☐ 56–65 ☐ 65+

Marital Status: ☐ Single ☐ Married ☐ Widowed ☐ Divorced

When it comes to learning, which medium is your favourite:

☐ Books ☐ Tapes ☐ CDs ☐ MP3 ☐ Video ☐ DVD

Number of Christian books you purchased in last year: ☐ 1–5 ☐ 5–10 ☐ 10+

Do you listen/watch: ☐ UCB ☐ Premier ☐ God TV ☐ other _____

What Christian magazines do you read regularly? _____

What was the last great Christian book you read? _____

Derek Prince Ministries–UK
Kingsfield • Hadrian Way
Baldock • SG7 6AN • UK

Tel: +44 (0)1462 492100
Web: www.dpmuk.org
Email: enquiries@dpmuk.org
Reg Charity No. 327763

This is an introductory offer for those not already on our mailing list   B46RC